Pebble® Plus

MILITARY MACHINES

MILITARY ROBOTS

by Barbara Alpert

Consulting Editor: Gail Saunders-Smith, PhD

Consultant: Raymond L. Puffer, PhD
Historian, Ret.
Edwards Air Force Base History Office

CAPSTONE PRESS
a capstone imprint

Pebble Plus is published by Capstone Press,
1710 Roe Crest Drive, North Mankato, Minnesota 56003.
www.capstonepub.com

 Books published by Capstone Press are manufactured with paper
containing at least 10 percent post-consumer waste.

Library of Congress Cataloging-in-Publication Data
Alpert, Barbara.
  Military robots / by Barbara Alpert.
      p. cm.—(Pebble plus. Military machines)
  Includes bibliographical references and index.
  Summary: "Simple text and full-color photographs describe various military robots"—Provided by publisher.
    ISBN 978-1-4296-7573-4 (library binding)
    ISBN 978-1-4296-7884-1 (paperback)
  1. Robotics—Military applications—Juvenile literature. 2. Armed Forces—Robots—Juvenile literature. I. Title.
  UG450.A47 2012
  623—dc23   2011021657

Editorial Credits
Erika L. Shores, editor; Kyle Grenz, designer; Kathy McColley, production specialist

Photo Credits
Getty Images/John Moore, 5, Wally Santana-Pool, 21
Newscom/ZUMA KPA/Dan Herrick-KPA, 11
Photo courtesy of Northrop Grumman Corporation, 19
U.S. Marine Corps photo by LCPL Patrick Green, 17
U.S. Navy photo by MC1 Brian A. Goyak, 13, MC1 Miguel Angel Contreras, 15, MC3 Kenneth G. Takada, 7, 9,
    PH1 Bart A. Bauer, cover, PH2 Daniel J. McLain, 19

Artistic Effects
Shutterstock: Hitdelight

Note to Parents and Teachers

The Military Machines series supports national standards related to science, technology, and
society. This book describes and illustrates military robots. The images support early readers
in understanding the text. The repetition of words and phrases helps early readers learn new
words. This book also introduces early readers to subject-specific vocabulary words, which are
defined in the Glossary section. Early readers may need assistance to read some words and to
use the Table of Contents, Glossary, Read More, Internet Sites, and Index sections of the book.

Printed in the United States of America in North Mankato, Minnesota.
052012   006702R

Table of Contents

What Are
Military Robots? 4

Parts of
Military Robots........... 6

Robots on Duty........... 12

Military Machines 20

Glossary........................22
Read More 23
Internet Sites.................23
Index............................24

What Are Military Robots?

Military robots are powerful machines. They do important jobs to keep military men and women safe.

Parts of Military Robots

Battery-powered computers run most robots. Soldiers control the robots from a distance. Soldiers often use a joystick to move robots in all directions.

Most ground robots have treads like tanks. They travel over all kinds of surfaces. Some robots even climb stairs.

treads

Robots carry tools and weapons. They use cameras to gather information. Robots with weapons can shoot at enemies.

camera

machine gun

cameras

Robots on Duty

The Talon is light enough

for soldiers to carry.

It tosses grenades,

shoots rockets, and

takes apart bombs.

The PackBot is smaller than the Talon. It looks under cars and through windows. It checks for bombs and other dangers.

Gladiators look like mini tanks.
The Gladiator weighs
1,600 pounds (726 kilograms).
Gladiators drive on wheels
or treads.

Unmanned aerial robots can be small like toys or big like airplanes. They fly over enemies and take pictures. They act as spies in the sky.

Military Machines

Military robots save lives by going into dangerous places. These machines deserve a medal!

Glossary

aerial—of or in the air; an aerial robot flies

grenade—a small bomb that can be thrown or launched

joystick—a lever used to control the movement of an object

robot—a machine that can do work and is operated by remote control or a computer

tread—a series of deep grooves and bumps

unmanned—drives or flies without a person onboard

Read More

Hyland, Tony. *Robot World.* Fast Facts. Mankato, Minn.: Sea-to-Sea Publications, 2012.

Jefferis, David. *Robot Warriors.* Robozones. New York: Crabtree Pub. Company, 2007.

White, Steve. *Military Robots.* High-Tech Military Weapons. New York: Children's Press, 2007.

Internet Sites

FactHound offers a safe, fun way to find Internet sites related to this book. All of the sites on FactHound have been researched by our staff.

Here's all you do:

Visit *www.facthound.com*

Type in this code: 9781429675734

Check out projects, games and lots more at
www.capstonekids.com

23

Index

bombs, 12, 14

cameras, 10

climbing, 8

computers, 6

flying, 18

Gladiators, 16

grenades, 12

joysticks, 6

PackBots, 14

rockets, 12

spies, 18

stairs, 8

Talons, 12, 14

tanks, 8, 16

tools, 10

treads, 8, 16

unmanned aerial robots, 18

weapons, 10, 12

Word Count: 173
Grade: 1
Early-Intervention Level: 20

2.5

Pts 0.5